CW00622094

HEALTH CARE
for
BIRDS

HEALTH CARE *for* BIRDS

The essential quick-reference guide

TIM HAWCROFT

BVSc (Hons), MACVSc, MRCVS

RINGPRESS

RINGPRESS

Published by Ringpress Books Ltd,
Spirella House, Bridge Road,
Letchworth, Herts, SG6 4ET, United Kingdom.

Discounts available for bulk orders
Contact the Special Sales Manager at
the above address. Telephone (0462) 674177

Distributed to the Book Trade in the United Kingdom by
Bookpoint Ltd.
39 Milton Park, Abingdon, Oxon OX14 4TD
Telephone 0235 835001

First Published 1994
© 1994 TIM HAWCROFT

ISBN 0 948955 68 6

Printed and bound in Singapore by Tien Wah Press

CONTENTS

INTRODUCTION

The spectacular plumage of many birds, their songs and habitual activity, give delight and treasured moments of relaxation to innumerable people throughout the world. Furthermore, their presence is vital to the continuing harmony and balance of our planet's ecology.

In today's world there has been an upsurge of interest in the protection, preservation and ecological significance of bird life: there are more active wildlife organisations for the protection and safety of birds; bird clubs have increased in number and membership; and more and more people are keeping birds in cages and aviaries for breeding purposes, and as pets.

This book is designed for all bird lovers and caring persons who want to know how to help a bird that is injured or sick, or want to update and extend their knowledge of First Aid for the bird. The know-how in this book, combined with experience, will give the reader confidence and skill to administer First Aid to a sick or injured bird.

The common causes of injury or illness in birds are storms, attacks by animals and other birds, pesticide poisons, cage and aviary accidents, thoughtless aggression (for example, duck shooting) and neglect and carelessness in the management of pet birds. The injury or illness sustained may range from fractures and collapse to bleeding and wounds.

Usually, injury or illness requires some form of First Aid, even if this means just giving some comfort to the bird. Should you have any doubt about the bird's condition or the treatment required, consult your veterinarian who will use diagnostic skills to recommend the appropriate treatment and give you general advice.

Saving a life, restoring a bird to health, arresting a worsening condition or giving a bird in distress some comfort and compassion is a rewarding and worthwhile experience.

THE CONCEPT OF FIRST AID

When a bird is hurt or sick, many people do not know how to help. It may be because they do not know how to approach and handle a bird or they do not know how to administer First Aid.

First Aid is not a new concept. Bird owners and others have been practising it for generations. First Aid information has been passed around mainly by word of mouth, but in recent times the media, authors, veterinarians and bird clubs have been disseminating it. The most practical understanding of the term is in its literal interpretation: it is the *First* Aid, help or treatment that is given to an injured or sick bird.

Minor, uncomplicated problems, such as hypothermia (low body temperature) and simple wounds, may only need a single treatment or, at the most, repetitions of it. The treatment starts and finishes on-site or at home.

Serious and life-threatening injuries and illness, such as major fractures, shock and poisoning, need not only immediate First Aid but require further treatment by a veterinarian.

When an injury or illness occurs at home or, for example, on a roadway, there is usually no veterinarian present. Whatever First Aid is given depends on the knowledge, skill, initiative and confidence of the owner or onlooker and the nature of the bird's injury or sickness. First Aid may range from something very simple, such as comforting the bird, to assessing its condition, perhaps moving it to safety, and then giving it the treatment thought necessary at the time.

Remember that *First* Aid is the first treatment and whatever treatment you can give is better than none at all.

HOW TO USE THIS BOOK

Familiarise yourself with the book's design, the location of various sections and their content. In doing so, you will be able to refer to the book for information in a calm, confident and speedy manner, especially in emergency situations. For ease of reference, we have set out the techniques, injuries and illnesses in alphabetical order. A detailed index in the back of the book will quickly guide you to the information you need.

Of course, the information you will require will depend on your situation and your knowledge. You will have to use your own judgment to determine your course of action.

If you are in a situation where a bird requires First Aid and you are unsure of the action you should take, we suggest you refer to the following sections in this order:
1. First Aid Priorities (see page 13)
2. The Injured or Ill Bird (see page 21)
3. When to Call Your Veterinarian (see page 32)
4. First Aid for Injuries and Illness (see page 48)

These sections offer practical guidance and back-up information so that you can determine what procedure to adopt to treat a particular injury or illness.

Although this book will serve you well in an emergency situation, it is best to be prepared. The purpose of the First Aid Kit section is to prompt you to set up a First Aid kit of your own. Likewise, the section on Accident Prevention is there to remind you of the old adage: prevention is better than cure.

To achieve competence in any activity involving skill, you must practise. The sections dealing with the Injured or Ill Bird and Techniques You Should Know contain procedures you should learn. The more you practise and the closer that practice is to reality, the more proficient and confident you will be when facing a real-life situation.

IMPORTANT
Always keep your veterinarian's telephone number handy.

FIRST AID KIT

• Store the First Aid kit in a suitable container, readily accessible, portable and marked for easy identification.

• Clean any soiled instruments after use and if necessary restock the kit.

• Every six months check the kit to see that everything is in good working order; for example, test the torch (flashlight) batteries.

• The kit should include the following items:

- Antibiotic powder

- Antiseptic wash

- Cotton buds (swabs)

- Eye dropper

- Ferric chloride

- Gauze swabs

- Hydrogen peroxide 1%

- Mercurochrome (antiseptic solution)

- Paraffin oil

- Roll of cottonwool (absorbent cotton)

- Roll of adhesive bandage (2.5cm (1in) wide)

- Roll of gauze bandage (2.5cm (1in) wide)

- Scissors (sharp, pointed, 10cm (4in) long)

- Syringe (plastic, 10ml)

- Thermometer (same as for human use)

- Tincture of iodine (anti-bacterial, anti-fungal solution)

- Torch (flashlight)

- Tweezers (forceps)

- Vetwrap bandaging tape

Previous page:
Correctly spaced bars should not allow a bird's head to poke through. The bird may be injured in the panic to gain release.

FIRST AID PRIORITIES

• Keep calm and work methodically.
• Assess whether injury or illness is life-threatening.

1. Life-threatening injuries or illness

• First treat life-threatening injuries or illness showing such signs as:
- Severe bleeding or blood flowing freely from a wound.
- Collapse.
• In such cases, administering immediate First Aid has top priority, but call the veterinarian as soon as possible.

2. Non-life-threatening injuries or illness accompanied by severe pain

• Next treat injuries or illness that are causing distress or pain but are not life-threatening. For example:
- Fracture.
- Diarrhea.
- Vomiting.
• Your treatment concerns preventing the injury or illness from worsening and preparing the bird for transportation to the veterinarian.

3. Minor injuries or illness

• Injuries such as a slight abrasion or minor cut come last in the order of priorities for treatment.
• Treat the bird at home if you know how.
• Take the bird to the veterinarian if the injury or illness does not improve or if the condition worsens.

Caution

• A bird may be in shock as a result of the injury or illness, and excessive handling. Furthermore, if a bird in shock is given intensive treatment and/or handling, the

Opposite: A well-designed and constructed aviary plays a significant part in preventing accidents and illnesses.

Below: A slippery perch may lead to injury. A tree branch is an excellent choice.

bird may collapse and die on the spot.
• In a life-threatening injury or illness, simultaneously treat the bird for shock (see page 86) and for the injury or illness.
• The treatment of lower priority injuries and illnesses (non-life-threatening) should be delayed for two to three hours if the bird is in shock. This delay will allow time for the bird to be treated for shock (see page 86) and to recover before being treated for the initial injury or illness.

ACCIDENT AND ILLNESS PREVENTION

• Never allow a tame bird to be free in a moving car. The bird could be very easily frightened and fly onto the driver, thereby creating a dangerous situation.

• Drive with caution when approaching a flock or community of ground birds on or near the roadway. The birds might mistime their flight in trying to avoid the car.

• Do not leave live electrical cords in an exposed situation in the home. If you have a tame bird with a powerful beak and that bird is allowed to roam freely, the bird could bite through the outside covering of an exposed cord and receive an electric shock.

• If you are spraying insecticide or household sprays inside or outside the house, make sure the spray does not invade the bird's cage or aviary.

• A well-designed and constructed cage or aviary plays a significant part in preventing and thereby reducing the incidence of accidents and illnesses amongst caged birds.
- An aviary can be built with two skins of wire mesh, about 10cm (4in) apart, that will protect birds against attacks from predators such as cats and some wild birds that can cause deep wounds, shock or even death.
- Wire bars are usually used in cages. Sometimes these are coated with a zinc compound which, if ingested, may cause zinc poisoning.
- The size of the holes in the mesh or the space between the bars must be considered so that there is no chance of the head of a contained bird poking through and the bird being injured in the panic to gain release.

- Birds fly horizontally or swerve upwards or downwards. It is therefore more important to consider the length of a cage rather than the height. Caged birds that do not have enough room to fly, even for a very short distance, may suffer from debility, boredom and stress.
- To help make cleaning easier, the bottom of a cage should have a removable sliding tray and an aviary should have a sloping concrete floor. Each should be cleaned regularly to avoid dampness or parasites and other infections developing in the debris of droppings, scattered seed, seed husks and other waste food that would otherwise accumulate. Such debris may lead to health problems such as diarrhea, weight loss, debility and feather loss.
- Birds need some sunlight for vitamin D production. Aviaries should be constructed in a way that allows exposure to sunlight but also provides a shade area to which birds can retreat from the sun and heat and for protection from the rain and wind. In a cold climate, aviaries may need to be insulated otherwise hypothermia and respiratory problems may develop. These principles also apply to the positioning of cages near open and closed windows where the use of a cover can help.

• Careful consideration should be given to the fittings of the cage or aviary. All birds need perches, drinking and food vessels and provision against extremes in temperature.
- Whatever the perch, it should be cleaned regularly to reduce the incidence of parasites and infection.
- A slippery perch may cause a bird to be unstable while perching. Some bird owners have tried to correct this problem by providing a perch encased in fine sandpaper, which in turn can be the cause of a problem known as bumblefoot. The best kind of perch is one taken from a branch of a tree similar to the one where the bird perches in the wild. A branch or branches of varying diameter allows a bird to choose the thickness which suits best.

Right: Food and water should be placed in suitable containers, not placed under perches, and checked daily for cleanliness.

Right: A cage too small for the size of the bird may cause the bird to become bored or stressed.

Opposite: Good perches have non-slippery surfaces, are of suitable diameter, and should be cleaned regularly.

18

The uneven surface of the branch makes it easier for the bird to grip and perch comfortably. A perch that is too small in diameter is the cause of cramping.

- Fouled water and food, and droppings are a source of disease. The floor of the cage can be kept clean by covering with newspaper, which is changed daily. Food and water should be placed in suitable containers, not placed under perches, and checked daily for cleanliness.

- A cage should be provided with a cover made of a material that does not shed easily. Loose threads are liable to tangle around the bird's toes and cut off circulation. The cover can protect the bird from heat stress (due to too much sunlight), hypothermia (from too much cold) and attack from predators, especially at night.

- A lone bird in a cage may suffer boredom and, as a consequence, may self-mutilate and spend time feather-plucking. The owner should provide entertainment in the form of appropriate equipment such as a ladder, mirror, bells and a swinging perch placed in the cage. Just as the bird provides company for the owner, the owner should provide some company for the bird in talking, whistling, stroking or even allowing the bird out of the cage into a safe room for a short time.

• The location of the cage or aviary is important. Birds should not be exposed to draughts that may aggravate respiratory problems. Sudden, loud noises or the fear of attack by predators may induce a state of stress or shock. When frightened, a bird's instinctive reaction is to take flight. In a 'fright-flight' situation, a caged bird could damage itself against the cage wire.

• Many accidents and illnesses can be prevented by providing good management covering such areas as parasite control, nutrition and cleanliness.

THE INJURED OR ILL BIRD

Catching, Handling, Assessing, Transporting

Catching a caged bird may be difficult or easy according to the bird's temperament, injury or illness, and the structure of the cage.

CATCHING
AND
HANDLING

Small bird in a small cage

Bird in a Cage

• Place the cage in a small room, for example, the laundry. Close all windows and doors in case the bird evades your grasp and escapes from the cage.
• Remove all objects from the cage, such as perches, swings and feeders, as they may get in your way when you are catching the bird.
• Small birds such as canaries and budgerigars are easy to catch on the floor of the cage or while gripping the wire.
• A trained bird may hop onto your finger. If this happens, stroke the bird gently then cup your hand firmly (not too tightly nor too loosely) around the wings and body of the bird, with the head between your thumb and index finger. This grip will control the head and so prevent the bird from biting (see page 26).
• If the bird is not trained, talk reassuringly while herding the bird slowly into a corner of the cage. Grasp the bird from behind in the same manner as described for a trained bird.
• Remove the bird from the cage for examination, treatment, transport to your veterinarian or for rehousing in a new cage or aviary.

Opposite: Catching a trained bird can be easy. The bird may just hop onto your finger.

Right: Small birds are easy to catch on the floor of a cage or while gripping the wire.

Below: After catching a bird with an aviary net, hold the opening of the net flat against the wire netting of the aviary to prevent the bird escaping.

Large bird in a large cage

• As for the small bird, place the cage in a small, escape-proof room and remove all objects from the cage.
• Check whether the cage door is large enough to allow your hand to reach the innermost part of the cage. If not, dismantle a section of the cage, such as the floor, in order to give you adequate access.
• Some birds may bite when caught. To reduce the possibility of being bitten wear a suitable glove. An effective alternative is to hold a towel in the hand to cushion the bite or to throw it over and cover the bird.
• The bird's head can be controlled by grasping the head between the thumb and index finger with the palm of the hand resting on the bird's back. The legs and wings can be controlled by wrapping the other hand around them, thus preventing the wings from being damaged and the feet injuring the handler (see page 30).

Bird free in a room or aviary

• Before attempting the catch, allow the bird to settle. A bird settled in a corner is easier to catch.
• Approach slowly and quietly but confidently, with a towel held spread out between your hands.
• When close, throw the towel over the bird and immediately tuck it in under the body. In this situation, a bird usually remains calm and still.
• Put your hand on top of the towel, and quickly feel for the bird's head under the towel. If the bird is to be transported, hold the bird's head between the thumb and index finger, then lift the bird, still enclosed in the towel, and place in a suitable container (see page 29). If you wish to examine the bird, pull the towel back to reveal one part of the bird at a time, beginning with the head.
• Alternatively, the bird can be caught with an aviary net similar to a butterfly net. Once the bird has been caught, hold the opening of the net flat against the wire netting of the aviary to prevent the bird escaping (see page 22).

Bird escaped outdoors from a cage in the home

• If the bird has a mate, place the mate in a cage outside the open window or door of the home. If the escaped bird returns, encourage the bird to come inside by bringing the caged mate just inside the door or window. If the bird comes inside, close the door or window and proceed to catch the bird (see page 24).
• If the bird has no mate, wait for the bird to settle in a tree or shrub and attempt to saturate the bird with a strong jet of water from a hose. Chances of success are minimal.

• Wild birds are difficult to catch unless they are ill or injured.
• Difficulty in catching will be directly related to the size of the bird and the nature of the injury or illness. The bird may be caught by:
- Hand.
- Using a bird net.
- Using a towel to throw over the bird. Under the towel, the bird should become quiet and calm thereby not causing further injury to itself or injury to you.
• The handler can take the following precautions to prevent injury once the bird is caught and under control:
- A beak can be taped with adhesive, electrician's tape or an elastic band (see page 31). Plasticine, for example, can be pushed onto the sharp point of the beak.
- Sharp, strong claws can puncture or tear the skin of a handler. Immobilise the claws by binding the legs together or allow the claws to grip a stick or some suitable object (see page 31). Bind the claws to the stick with a suitable material, such as Vetwrap, which is a self-adhesive bandage.

Wild Bird

• Any obvious bleeding (see page 37) or signs of shock (see page 86) should be treated before handling the bird to assess the bird's condition in detail.

ASSESSING THE BIRD'S CONDITION

25

Left: To avoid being bitten, a strong glove should be used when attempting to catch a large bird.

Left: A towel can be used to control a bird's wings and legs.

Opposite: Hold a small bird by cupping your hand firmly around the wings and body of the bird, with the head between your thumb and index finger.

27

• Excessive handling of a bird in shock may cause death.

• Allow 2 to 3 hours recovery time from shock before assessing the bird.

Assessment procedure

First, stand a short distance away and visually examine the bird, looking for:

- *Symmetry or asymmetry*. For example, a drooping wing. Indicates possible fracture (see page 61).

- *Eye discharge*. Indicates possible conjunctivitis (see page 52).

- *Nasal discharge*. Indicates possible respiratory infection (see page 75).

- *Head tilt*. Indicates possible concussion (see page 52).

- *Bird huddled*. Often on the bottom of the cage. This is a general sign of illness.

- *Abnormal breathing*. Indicates possible respiratory infection (see page 75).

- *Posture*. Head turned towards the wing with eyes partly closed. This is a general sign of illness.

- *Fluffed out feathers*. This is a general sign of illness.

- *Feathers stained*. Staining just above the nostrils indicates a possible respiratory infection (see page 75).

- *Feathers around the head*. Matted with tacky mucus and partially digested seed or food. Indicates vomiting (see page 88).

- *Feathers around the vent*. Stained or matted with droppings, or droppings of a fluid-like consistency on the bottom of the cage. Indicates diarrhea (see page 56).

- *Feather loss*. Indicates possible underlying wound (see page 89).

Next carefully and methodically examine the bird physically:

- Begin with the head, checking for signs of abrasion, beak fractures, eye injuries, unequal pupil size, mouth and tongue problems, which may indicate possible concussion (see page 52).

- Check for unequal pupil size which may indicate possible concussion (see page 52).

- Check the neck for feather loss or feathers matted together, which may indicate an underlying wound (see page 89).

- Feel the body, particularly the breast (keel) bone and breast (pectoral) muscles. If the breast bone is prominent and the muscles are wasted, starvation (see page 86) or some chronic illness is indicated. Feathers lost or matted together may indicate a wound (see page 89).

- Examine each wing. Take hold of the wingtip and pull it away from the body, to extend the full wing so that the bones and joints can be felt for possible fractures and dislocations. Wounds or bleeding may be detected. In practice, fractures are more easily detected from the underside of the wing (see page 35).

- Lastly, feel the legs for fractures (see page 61). The bones in the leg are easier to feel if the leg is extended.

TRANSPORTING THE BIRD

• An injured or ill bird may be transported to the veterinarian or wildlife centre in such containers as:

- A cage with a cover.

- A cardboard box punched with a few airholes and lined with towelling.

- A sock.

- A sack with a hole just large enough for the bird's head to poke through.

• All these containers will provide some warmth and subdued lighting, thereby calming the bird and alleviating shock. Your choice will depend on availability of materials and the size of the bird.

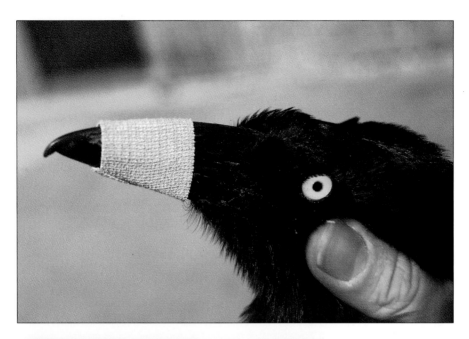

Above: A bird's beak can be taped shut to avoid injury to the handler.

Left: Sharp claws can be immobilised by allowing the bird to grip a suitable object. Bind the claws to the object with a suitable material such as Vetwrap.

Opposite: Control a large bird by grasping the head between thumb and index finger with the palm of the hand resting on the bird's back. Wrap the other hand around the legs and wings.

31

WHEN TO CALL YOUR VETERINARIAN

The following information may serve as a guide if you are uncertain when to call your veterinarian.

CALL IMMEDIATELY

- **Bleeding**. Will not stop. Apply pressure to stop the bleeding (see page 37).
- **Blood in vomit and/or diarrhea.** Evidence of blood; fluid diarrhea (see page 56).
- **Burns.** Fairly extensive (see page 51).
- **Collapse or loss of balance.** Overreaction to external stimuli; depression; staggering; walking in circles; down/ unable to get up; tremor; rigidity; coma. Could indicate concussion (see page 52) or convulsion (see page 54).
- **Poisoning.** Chemical or plant — retain for veterinarian to identify type of poisoning (see page 79).
- **Serious injury.** Puncture wound, especially to eye, chest or abdomen; or a deep, gaping laceration with or without bone exposed (see page 89); fracture (see page 61).
- **Severe breathing difficulty.** Distressed, gaspy, noisy breathing (see page 75).
- **Straining continually.** Attempting to pass droppings. Could indicate constipation (see page 53) or egg bound bird (see page 57).
- **Uncontrollable itching.** Continual, uncontrollable scratching and/or pecking at the skin; skin broken and bleeding.

CALL SAME DAY

- **Appetite loss.** Not eating; depressed in conjunction with other signs, such as laboured breathing, diarrhea.
- **Breathing difficulty.** Laboured breathing; rapid and shallow breathing with or without cough (see page 75).

32

• **Egg bound.** Straining; depression; abdominal distension (see page 57).
• **Eye problems.** Eyelids partially or completely closed; cornea (surface of eye) cloudy, opaque or bluish-white in colour (see page 59).
• **Foreign body swallowed.** Better for veterinarian to assess rather than wait for a possible life-threatening situation to develop.
• **Hypothermia.** Low body temperature (see page 74).
• **Injuries.** Not urgent, but liable to become infected; a small cut through full thickness of skin; puncture wound (see page 89).
• **Self-mutilation.** Pecking; scratching; feather loss; skin red and inflamed.
• **Severe diarrhea.** Motion (stool) fluid and profuse or frequent; abdominal pain or straining (see page 56).
• **Swelling.** Hot, hard and painful or discharging.

• **Appetite loss.** Not eating; no other sign or symptom.
• **Diarrhea.** Motion (stool) is softer than normal; no sign of blood; no indication of abdominal pain or straining (see page 56).
• **Itching.** Moderate; no damage to the skin by self-mutilation.
• **Thirst.** Excessive drinking.
• **Vomiting.** On two or three occasions with no other symptoms (see page 88).

WAIT 24 HOURS BEFORE CALLING

Right: A bird fluffed up with the head turned towards the wing and eyes partially closed is displaying signs of general illness.

Below: Fluffed-out feathers are a general sign of illness.

Left: A small injured or ill bird can be transported in a sock which will provide some warmth to help alleviate shock.

Below: To examine a wing, take hold of the wingtip and pull it away from the body, extending the wing to full length.

TECHNIQUES YOU SHOULD KNOW

Bleeding — How to Stop

• The blood volume of a bird is relatively small, the average being 9ml (approximately 2 teaspoons) per 100g (3.5oz) body weight. A budgerigar weighing 30g (1oz) would have a total blood volume of about 3ml (approximately ½ teaspoon).
• Injured birds are not prone to bleeding profusely. Birds have a very efficient blood-clotting mechanism. As their blood volume is relatively small, they cannot afford to lose any significant amount. Twelve drops of blood would represent approximately 20 per cent of a budgerigar's total blood volume.
• Birds bleed more freely from a broken or cut nail, or the beak, than from a skin wound.
• Movement accelerates bleeding. Keep the bird still. Ideally, one person immobilises the bird while another person controls the bleeding (see page 21).

Bleeding from the Beak

• Immobilise the bird (see page 21).
• Using a cotton bud (swab), apply pressure to the site for approximately one minute. If not available, apply pressure with your finger, and preferably a gauze pad. Take care not to be bitten.
• If available, dip a cotton bud (swab) into liquid ferric chloride, then apply to the site of bleeding with pressure for 30 seconds (see page 38).
• Do not have excess ferric chloride on the cotton bud (swab), because any drips into the bird's mouth may burn the delicate mucous membrane.

Bleeding from a Nail

• Immobilise the bird (see page 21).
• Apply pressure to the point of bleeding with your fingertip or a cotton bud (swab) for approximately one minute.
• If available, dip a cotton bud (swab) into liquid ferric

chloride, then apply to the point of bleeding with pressure for about 30 seconds.

Bleeding Quill

• A growing feather has a blood vessel running up the shaft. Injury to the growing quill may result in excessive bleeding.
• Immobilise the bird (see page 21).
• Locate the damaged quill.
• Using a pair of tweezers (forceps) grasp the base of the quill tightly and quickly pluck it out.

Skin Wound

Below: Liquid ferric chloride can be applied to a bleeding beak with a cotton bud (swab).

• Skin wounds usually do not bleed freely.
• Immobilise the bird (see page 21).
• Apply pressure with your fingertip for one minute, or longer if necessary. Or use a clean wad of cloth if available.

Left: Liquid ferric chloride can be applied to a bleeding nail with a cotton bud (swab).

Below: To prevent a bird interfering with wounds, an Elizabethan collar can be made and fitted at home.

39

Elizabethan Collar — Making and Fitting

An Elizabethan collar is used to prevent a bird pecking itself, pulling out feathers, scratching or rubbing the head, or pecking a bandage or splint. Your veterinarian can supply you with a commercial type or you can make one (see page 39).

• Select a suitable sheet of firm plastic, for example, an ice-cream container or takeaway food container.
• Cut the plastic into a circular shape. The circle will have to be large enough so that when the bird's head is passed through a hole in the centre, the bird cannot take hold of the outer edge of the plastic with the beak.
• Cut into the circle in a straight line from the outside edge to the centre (radius). At the centre, cut a circular hole large enough to accommodate the bird's neck, taking into account that the feathers make the bird's neck look larger.
• Line the sharp edge of the neck hole with tape to prevent damage to the bird's skin.
• One person holds the bird (see page 21) while another fits the collar. If the neck hole is too large, reduce the size by overlapping the edges of the cut (radius). Once you are satisfied the collar is the right size, that is, the collar can be swivelled around the bird's neck fairly freely and will not come off, staple together the overlapping edges of the radius cut to secure the collar in place.

Caution

• After applying the collar, check to see that the bird can eat, drink and perch.
• Make certain that the bird cannot get a foot caught in the neck hole, between the neck and the collar.

Medicine — How to Administer

Medicine may be in the form of a medicated seed, powder, liquid, ointment, drops or injection. How the medicine is given and in what form depends on such factors as its type and palatability, the condition and temperament of the bird, and the owner's temperament. Administering medication in the feed is inefficient but is easier for those owners who do not wish to handle the bird.

• Medicated seeds are available commercially. The success of medicated seeds depends on the condition of the bird. Seriously injured or sick birds usually do not eat or eat very little. Also, this type of medicine is only suitable for grain-eating birds, such as budgerigars, canaries and cockatoos.

Administering Medicated Seed

• This is not a good method, because the amount of medication taken by the bird is in proportion to the amount of food consumed, which is usually determined by the medication's palatability and the nature of the bird's injury or illness. In effect, the bird may be overdosed or underdosed.
• The powder can be made to stick to the seed by coating the seed with vegetable oil before adding the medicated powder.
• If the medicine is in liquid form, the seed can be soaked in the liquid overnight so that it is well impregnated before feeding the bird.

Powders and Liquids in the Feed

• The bird may be overdosed or underdosed according to the amount of water consumed. When using this method, make sure the bird is drinking the medicated water. The palatability of the water can be improved by adding glucose or honey.

Powders and Liquids in the Drinking Water

41

Liquids by Eye Dropper or Syringe

• This form of administration requires you to be able to catch and restrain the bird (see page 21).
• Hold the bird from behind, with the head between your thumb and index finger and the palm of your hand and remaining fingers enclosing the body, wings and legs (see page 26).
• Turn your hand over so that the bird's head is tilted slightly backwards. This position will allow liquid from the eye dropper to run towards the back of the throat rather than towards the open mouth (beak).
• Hold the eye dropper or syringe in the other hand, and move the tip of it towards the bird's beak; the bird will automatically open the mouth to bite the tip.
• Quickly dribble the liquid, a drop at a time, into the mouth. If the bird does not swallow, tilt the head back a little more and dribble more liquid into the mouth. If you tilt the bird back too far and administer the liquid too quickly, the medicine may flow into the windpipe, causing the bird to splutter.

Crop Feeding

• This is an efficient, professional method of administering liquid medication using a plastic tube or a metal crop needle attached to a syringe. *Crop feeding should be left to your veterinarian or trained personnel,* who have the required special knowledge and skill.

Administration by Injection

• This is a route often taken by veterinarians. Injecting medication is quick, efficient and convenient and should be left to your veterinarian or trained personnel.

Administering Drops and Ointments

• **Eye drops.** With the bird's head held between your thumb and index finger (see page 21), tilt the head to the side so that the eye you are treating is uppermost. Holding the bottle of eyedrops in your other hand, put one drop directly onto the eyeball. Keep the bird's head tilted to the side for 20 seconds to prevent the eyedrops rolling out and being wasted.

Left: Liquids can be administered with a syringe. The bird should be held from behind with the head tilted slightly backwards.

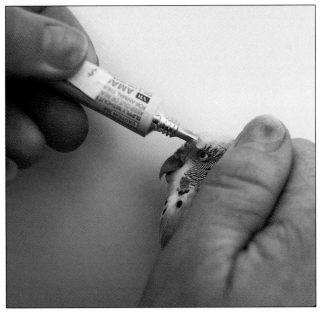

Left: When applying eye ointments, the bird's head should be held between thumb and forefinger with the head tilted to the side.

• **Eye ointment.** Many eye ointments are manufactured to be solid at room temperature and to melt at body temperature. In applying these ointments, use the same technique as for administering eye drops (see pages 42 and 43). Avoid using excess ointment to prevent contaminating the feathers around the eye, which may lead to excessive preening and self-mutilation.

Temperature — How to Check

Different species of birds have different body temperature ranges. The normal temperature for most birds ranges from 40°C (104°F) to 42°C (108°F). Birds lose body heat quickly when debilitated and may die from hypothermia (low body temperature). Those birds with a temperature less than 38°C (100°F) should be warmed until their normal temperature has been reached (see page 45). Birds also suffer from heatstroke (see page 73).

• Shake the mercury down to below 38°C (100°F) and smear the thermometer with a non-irritant lubricant, such as Vaseline.
• Insert the thermometer into the bird's cloaca (the cavity through which droppings and eggs are passed) to about 0.75cm (0.5in).
• Withdraw the thermometer after one to two minutes and check the reading.
• Clean the thermometer with disinfectant, and store in a suitable container.
• Wash your hands thoroughly.

Keep in mind

• A household clinical thermometer is only useful to measure a bird's normal temperature or below. Overheating has to judged by the symptoms displayed by the bird (see page 73).

Warming an Injured, Ill or Orphan Bird

A healthy, adult bird in its natural environment does not require an artificially warm environment. Warmth, however, is often critical for the survival of an injured, ill or orphan bird (see page 76).

Orphan bird

• Precocial (born covered in down) and altricial (born featherless) chicks should be housed in a cardboard box lined with shredded newspaper.
• Place a 40 watt light bulb above the box, sufficiently high to maintain the floor temperature within the box at 30° C (86°F) to 32°C (90°F).
• Check the temperature by placing a thermometer on the floor of the box directly under the bulb.
• Provide space for the chick to move away from the heat source to prevent overheating.
• As the chick becomes feathered, gradually reduce the temperature to 20°C (68°F) by moving the light bulb further away.

Sick, injured or shocked birds

• Place the bird in a suitably sized cardboard box or cage.
• If using a cardboard box, line with a towel or shredded newspaper and provide holes for ventilation.
• If a cage, cover the top and sides with a thick blanket or several towels.
• The cage or box can be heated by placing near an electric heater (be careful of high heat settings and placing the box too close to the heater), a 60 watt incandescent light bulb, or an electric heating pad or blanket. Make sure the bird cannot get access to any electric cord.
• Provide space for the bird to move away from the heat source to prevent overheating.

• Maintain the temperature within the cage or box at 30°C (86°F) to 32°C (90°F) until the bird has made a full recovery.

• Dry heat can cause dehydration. Increase the humidity by placing a shallow bowl of water in the cage or box, or between the heat source and the bird.

• Monitor the temperature in the cage or box regularly.

• When the bird is sufficiently warm, the feathers will be smooth and unruffled and the bird will be alert and active.

• If necessary, the body (cloacal) temperature can be checked (see page 44).

• Gradually reduce the environmental temperature to 20°C (68°F).

Opposite: A cardboard box, shredded newspaper and a light bulb can provide a warm environment for an injured, ill or orphan bird.

FIRST AID FOR INJURIES AND ILLNESS

Attack by Predators

Birds are often attacked by dogs and other birds but it is the cat that is the bird's greatest enemy, especially in the wild. Cats can inflict puncture wounds with their canine teeth and claws. These wounds may look neat and clean on the surface but under the skin the tissues may be badly torn or infected and the bones may be broken. Other wounds that may be inflicted by a cat include lacerations, feather loss, a damaged wing and shock.

Signs

- Shock (see page 86).
- Drooping wing (see page 68).
- Blood matted in feathers.
- Lameness (see page 61).

Action

- Minimal handling.
- Control any bleeding (see page 37).
- Treat for shock by placing the bird in a warm, quiet, dimly lit environment (see page 86).
- If the shock has not improved within approximately 3 hours, contact your veterinarian.
- When the bird's condition improves, treat any fractures (see page 61) or minor wounds.
- Using your fingers, carefully pluck the feathers away from the puncture wound.
- Clean the wound with 1% peroxide solution.
- If the wound appears to penetrate through the skin into underlying tissues, take the bird to the veterinarian who will administer antibiotics.

Burns

• Burns are usually caused by chemicals, electricity, heat and, in the case of wild birds, forest fires.
• Take the bird to your veterinarian. Deep or extensive burns require immediate veterinary attention.

Many household products such as chlorine can cause burns, mostly to the skin.

CHEMICAL BURN

• If on the skin, rinse gently with cold water followed by a wash with soap and warm water. Rinse thoroughly.

Action

Birds with powerful beaks, such as cockatoos, are more at risk because they can bite into an electrical cord.

ELECTRICAL BURN

• Turn off the power at the switch. If you are unable to reach the switch, use a dry, wooden or plastic stick to flick the plug out of the socket or the bird away from the source of the electricity.
• Treat the bird for shock (see page 86).
• Take the bird to your veterinarian.

Action

Extensive burns are associated with shock (see page 86), fluid loss (dehydration) (see page 55) and infection.

HEAT BURN

• Immediately run cold water gently on the burn from a hose or tap; if ice is readily available, apply for 10 to 15 minutes; or immerse the burnt area in a basin filled with water and ice. Keep the rest of the bird's body warm to counteract shock.
• Dry the area by dabbing gently. Do not rub as you may break the delicate surface of the bird's skin.
• Deep or extensive burns require quick veterinary attention.

Action

Concussion

Head injuries occur when wild birds fly into glass
windows or frightened caged birds fly into the cage wire.

Signs

One or more signs may be exhibited:
- Depression.
- Loss of balance.
- Circling with or without head tilted.
- Weakness of wings and legs.
- Convulsions.

Action

- Possible shock should be counteracted by keeping the
bird warm and quiet (see page 45).
- Confine the bird in a box padded with a piece of
towelling and place in a quiet, secluded area with air
temperature at approximately 30°C (86°F).
- If the bird is confined to a cage, lower the perches
and remove any toys and the water container.
- If the bird is unable to perch, cover the floor with
shredded newspaper.
- Contact your veterinarian.

Conjunctivitis

The conjunctiva is the membrane lining the inside of
the eyelids. Conjunctivitis is an inflammation and/or
infection of that membrane. The symptoms are easily
detected in a bird.

Signs

- Eyelids stuck together.
- Pus oozing from the corners of the eyelids.
- Dry pus adhered to the edges of the eyelids.

Action

- Warm bathing and gentle parting of the eyelids.
- Be careful not to pull the eyelids apart too abruptly because you may damage the rims.
- While bathing, wipe away any discharge adhering to the lids. This helps to prevent the eyelids sealing together again.
- Keep the bird out of the wind and direct sunlight.
- If the discharge is heavy and/or continuous see your veterinarian, who will prescribe an appropriate eye ointment/drops.

Caution

- There are numerous eye ointments available commercially, all of which have a specific purpose. Do not use them indiscriminately for conjunctivitis, because some can worsen certain conditions. For example, if there is an ulceration of the cornea (surface of the eyeball) and it is incorrectly treated, the result may be a permanently damaged eye or even blindness.

Constipation

Signs

- The bird shows signs of straining, depression and abdominal distension, similar signs to those when a bird is egg bound.

Action

- Remove any droppings (faeces) from the area around the vent and pluck any feathers that are heavily contaminated from droppings.
- Give a few drops of paraffin oil orally.
- Lubricate the vent with a non-irritant lubricant or paraffin oil.

Convulsions

Causes

- Convulsions may be caused by poisoning, head injury, infection, vitamin B deficiency, low blood calcium or sugar levels.

Signs

One or more signs may be exhibited:
- Shaking, twitching.
- Lying on side, paddling with legs and fluttering wings.
- Violent floundering.

Action

- Confine the bird in a padded box and place in a quiet, secluded area with air temperature at approximately 30°C (86°F) (see page 45).
- If the bird is confined to a cage, lower the perches and remove any toys and the water container.
- If the bird is unable to perch, cover the floor with shredded newspaper.
- Contact your veterinarian.

Crop Impaction

- The crop is the special pouch-like enlargement of the gullet of most birds in which food undergoes partial preparation for digestion.
- This problem is usually found among greedy feeders. The distended crop may be seen and felt under the skin.

Action

- Give 2 drops of paraffin oil orally.
- Massage the crop gently to assist in movement of the impacted mass.

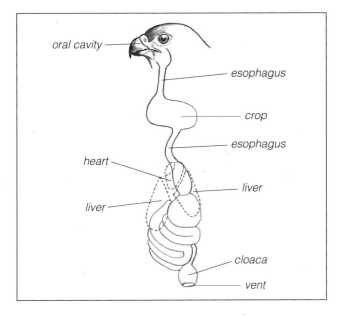

oral cavity

esophagus

crop

esophagus

heart

liver

liver

cloaca

vent

Left: The crop is the special pouch-like enlargement of a bird's gullet.

Dehydration

Dehydration in birds may be due to:
• Inadequate supply of water.
• Inability to drink due to damaged beak or tongue, infected throat or damaged neck.
• Vomiting and/or diarrhea.

Causes

Lethargy; poor appetite; hard, dry droppings; sunken eyes and skin that does not slide easily over the breast (keel) bone can all be signs of dehydration.

Signs

• Handle the bird gently and as little as possible.
• Give an electrolyte solution from a syringe or eye dropper. Obtain a commercial electrolyte solution or powder from your veterinarian. If unavailable, make up a solution of one teaspoon of glucose substitute powder to 100mls (½ cup) of water.

Action

• Administer the solution at the rate of 1 to 2mls ($\frac{1}{3}$ teaspoon) per 100gms (4ozs) of body weight. The following body weights may serve as a guide:
- Canary 15—30gm (0.5—1oz)
- Budgerigar 30—55gm (1—2oz)
- Lovebird 50—60gm (2—2.2oz)
- Pigeon 300—450gm (10.5—16oz)

• Take the bird to your veterinarian for administration of fluids by crop feeding or by injection if you are unable to manage the bird.

Diarrhea

• The normal droppings of birds are made up of three components: a clear colourless liquid (urine), a solid white substance (uric acid) and a solid dark substance (faeces).
• The consistency of the droppings will vary according to the species of bird. Seed-eating birds have drier, firmer droppings than nectar-eating birds, whose faeces are of a fluid consistency. Birds eating succulent green vegetables or plants will have softer, greener droppings.
• Stress caused by transportation or confinement in a small cage of a wild or aviary bird may cause the droppings to be of a more fluid consistency.
• Diarrhea in birds can be caused by an inadequate diet, worms, an infection or poisoning.

Signs

• The droppings are of a fluid-like consistency.
• The bird may be lethargic, fluffed-up and/or experience loss of appetite.
• The feathers around the vent may be stained or matted with faeces.

Actions

• Check to see that the diarrhea is not associated with a change of diet. There are numerous causes of diarrhea,

some of which can only be diagnosed in a veterinary laboratory examination of the droppings.
• Whilst the cause is being diagnosed, isolate the bird from other birds to prevent spread of infection.
• Keep the bird warm (see page 45), provide fluids to prevent dehydration, and temporarily remove the bird's food.

Prevention

• Isolate a bird immediately you notice the symptoms of diarrhea.
• Clean the cage or aviary and contents thoroughly with boiling water or an antiseptic wash.
• Wash your hands after treating a sick bird or cleaning a bird's cage to prevent possible infection of yourself and other birds.
• Wash all fruit, vegetables and plants thoroughly in water to remove any traces of pesticides before feeding to the bird.

Egg Bound

Causes

• The common causes are calcium deficiency, obesity or low body temperature.

Signs

• The bird shows signs of straining, depression, abdominal distension.

Action

• Warm the bird for 3 hours (see page 45).
• Lubricate the cloaca (the cavity from which droppings and eggs are passed) with Vaseline or some other suitable lubricant. Often the egg can be removed by manual manipulation.
• If lubrication and manual manipulation fails, drain the contents of the egg with a needle and syringe. The shell will collapse and can be removed manually with forceps or tweezers, or will be expelled in due course.

• Alternatively, your veterinarian will give the bird a calcium injection. If the egg is not expelled within 2 hours after the injection, your veterinarian will remove the egg surgically.

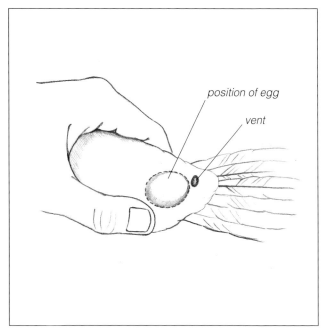

position of egg

vent

Right: An egg-bound bird will suffer swelling near the vent.

Right: An egg-bound bird will show signs of straining, depression and abdominal distension.

58

Eye Injuries

Any injury to the eyeball or eyelids should be regarded as serious and damage to the eyeball may lead to permanent blindness.

Action
• Seek veterinary attention immediately.
• Keep the eyelid(s) and/or eyeball moist by holding a wad of cottonwool (absorbent cotton) soaked in water over the eye.

CHLORINE BURN TO THE EYE
Because the eye is moist, chlorine will adhere to the eye, burning it and in some cases causing permanent damage or blindness.

Action
• Wash the eye immediately and repeatedly, using such techniques as:
- Flushing the eye with a syringe filled with clean water.
- Wiping the eye gently until clean with a cottonwool (absorbent cotton) ball saturated in water.
- Dripping water onto the eye from a saturated cottonwool (absorbent cotton) ball.
• Seek veterinary assistance quickly.

FOREIGN BODY IN THE EYE
Foreign bodies such as seed husks can cause permanent damage to the eye.

Action
• Wash the eye with copious amounts of water.
• Gently open and close the eyelids to work the foreign body towards the corner of the eyelids or to make it visible.
• If visible, carefully attempt to remove the foreign body by wiping the eye with moist cottonwool (absorbent cotton). In cases where the foreign body is accessible but adhering to the tissues, use tweezers (forceps) carefully.

• If unable to remove, or if after removal the bird is very uncomfortable, seek veterinary assistance.
• Seek veterinary assistance if the bird's eye is closed and you cannot identify the problem.

Fishhook Caught in Mouth

Caution

• Do not push or pull the hook.

Action

If the bird is quiet and the barbed end of the hook is protruding from the beak

• With an assistant holding the bird's head firmly (see page 21), cut off the barb of the hook using a pair of pliers or metal cutters, or cut the eye from the hook, whichever is more convenient.
• The remainder of the hook can then be removed readily.

If the bird is agitated or the barbed end of the hook is embedded in the membranous lining of the mouth

• Seek veterinary assistance.

Fishing Line Disappearing into Mouth

Caution

• Do not cut the line. It may be attached to a fishhook and could be of use to the veterinarian in locating and removing the hook.
• Prevent the bird from swallowing the line by tying it around the beak until the bird can be examined.

• Hold the bird (see page 21) and tilt the head backwards. The mouth will usually open.
• If the fishing line disappears into the back of the throat, gently pull the line.
• If it will not budge, do not persist in pulling.
• Seek veterinary assistance.

Action

Fractures

• The wing, leg and beak of the bird are the most common fracture sites. The more obvious types of fracture are:
- **Clean break.** A bone is broken in a simple, clean-cut break.
- **Multiple.** A bone is broken in two or more places.
- **Compound.** The broken end of a bone protrudes through the skin. This is a serious fracture because of the danger of infection.
• Successful mending of a broken bone depends on:
- The two broken ends being correctly opposed against one another.
- Immobilisation of the fractured bone until healing has taken place.
• The bones of small birds take about 2 to 3 weeks to heal; bones of larger birds take longer.
• If a bird is pecking at the bandage that immobilises a fracture, you may have to fit the bird with an Elizabethan collar (see page 40).
• Position all perches down near the bottom of the cage to keep the overall movement of the bird to a minimum.
• If in any doubt, confine the bird, treat for shock (see page 86) and transport to a veterinarian (see page 29).

• Leg misshapen.
• Leg held off the ground or perch.
• Difficulty in perching.

**LEG
FRACTURE
Signs**

• When fractured, the whole leg or most of it is often drawn up under the feathers. For examination, the leg has to be extended and exposed. The procedure involves two people, one to hold the bird, the other to locate, position and bandage the fracture.

Upper Leg Fracture

• The upper leg is usually not visible as it is covered by feathers. The bones in the upper leg are the femur and tibiotarsus (see diagram page 67).

• Treatment should be left to the veterinarian, who can X-ray the leg, determine the nature of the fracture and decide on the best method of immobilisation, for example, a plaster cast or pinning. The bird is anaesthetised for treatment.

• An alternative method of immobilisation is to use a sling (see diagram page 63):

Below: It is easier to examine for fractures if the leg is extended.

- For advice on holding the bird during the procedure, see page 21.

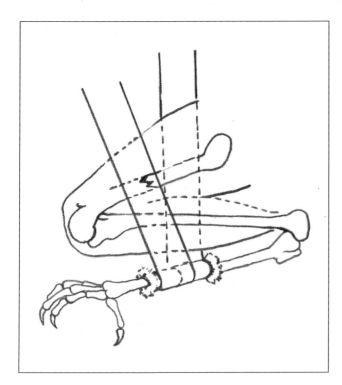

Left: A sling can be used to immobilise a fractured upper leg.

Left: Pass the sling under the wings to allow the bird to maintain balance and fly.

- Vetwrap, approximately 1cm (⅜in) wide, is a suitable bandage for a sling as it is self-adhesive.
- With the leg extended, wrap the lower leg, known as the tarsometatarsus bone (see diagram page 67), in wadding (soft, spongy material) to protect the skin against chafe and pressure.
- Pass the sling around the wadding two or three times, then around the body to draw the lower leg up into a natural flexed position firmly against the body.
- Pass the sling under the wings to allow the bird to maintain balance and fly.
- Check daily to see that the sling is keeping the leg in the flexed position.
- The sling is left on for 2 to 3 weeks, or longer if necessary.
• If the bird pecks and loosens the sling, apply an Elizabethan collar (see page 40).

Lower Leg Fracture

• The lower leg (tarsometatarsus bone) is visible and recognisable by its scaly appearance (see diagram page 67). If the tarsometatarsus bone is fractured, several methods are suggested for immobilisation and these are outlined below.

Action

Vetwrap bandage

• Vetwrap is easy to apply and readily adjusted and removed because of its self-adhesive characteristic.
• Extend the fractured leg. Firmly wrap a 1cm (⅜in) wide bandage around the full length of the tarsometatarsus bone several times. To secure good immobilisation, the fracture site should be in the middle of the bandage. If the fracture is towards one end of the tarsometatarsus bone, it will be necessary to extend the bandage.
• Leave the bandage in place for 2 to 3 weeks, or longer if necessary. (See page 66.)

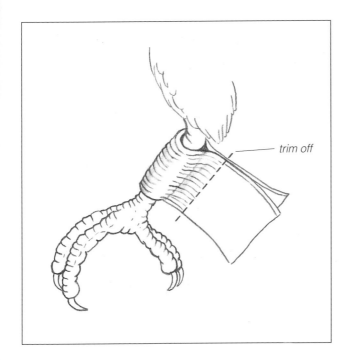

trim off

Left: Two to four pieces of adhesive bandage can be applied to immobilise a lower leg fracture.

Adhesive bandage

• Cut two to four pieces of adhesive bandage 2.5cm (1in) wide and 5cm (2in) in length to surround the leg. Lay one piece on top of the other so that they stick together and leave the top one with its sticky surface uncovered.

• Extend the fractured leg, place the middle of the sticky surface on the spot where the leg is fractured and fold the bandage around the leg so that the sticky surfaces meet together on the other side to form a firm-fitting, adhesive bandage cast around the leg (see diagram above). Trim off any unnecessary length of adhesive bandage.

• Leave in place for 2 to 3 weeks, or longer if necessary. If the skin is broken, see the veterinarian who will prescribe antibiotics to prevent infection.

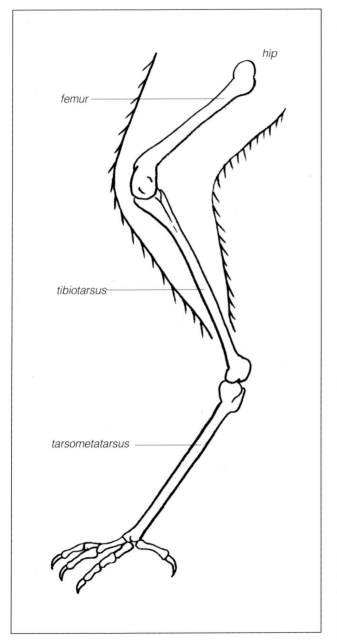

Left: A bird's leg is made up of three bones.

hip

femur

tibiotarsus

tarsometatarsus

Opposite: A Vetwrap bandage is firmly wrapped several times around the full length of the tarsometatarsus bone to immobilise a lower leg fracture.

Right: A drinking straw and wadding can be used to make an effective splint for a lower leg fracture.

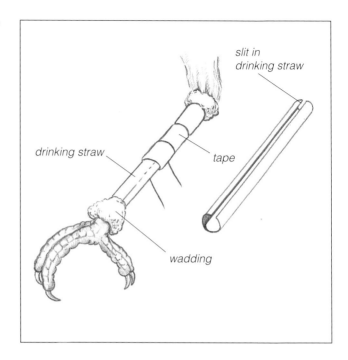

Splint

- First extend the leg and wrap the lower leg in wadding to protect the skin from pressure.
- Cut a drinking straw to a length that is shorter than the wadding so that the sharp ends do not cut into the skin.
- Slit the drinking straw lengthwise, fit it over the wadding then bandage over the straw with Vetwrap or adhesive bandage. Leave in place for 2 to 3 weeks or longer if necessary. (See diagram above.)
- Without removing the splint, check regularly to see that no pressure sores are developing at either end of the splint and there is no swelling of the foot.

WING FRACTURE

- Wing fractures within 0.5cm (¼ in) of the joints do not heal well; that is, the fractured bone ends do not unite or the joint becomes stiff, making flight impossible.

• Vetwrap bandage is recommended for use as it conforms to the shape of the body, is easy to adjust, does not stick and therefore does not damage the feathers when being removed.

• Do not apply the Vetwrap bandage too tightly as it may restrict the bird's breathing, nor too loosely as the bird will move the wing, thus preventing the fracture healing.

• Treatment involves two people, one to hold the bird (see page 21), the other to examine and locate the site of the fracture.

Signs

• A drooping wing.
• The bird stays on the ground or floor of the cage.
• If disturbed, the bird attempts to fly and is unsuccessful.

For a small bird

• Fold the fractured wing into its natural position. Wrap the bandage (about 2.5cm/1in wide) firmly over the wing and around the body but under the sound wing.

• Leave the bandage in place for 2 to 3 weeks, or longer if necessary.

• Alternatively, after folding the fractured wing into its natural position, wrap a bandage over both wings just behind where they are attached to the body, and continue the bandage under, up and around the body several times. Wrap another bandage around the body to secure the tips of the flight feathers. Prevent this bandage from slipping by joining it to the other bandage with strips of Vetwrap (see diagram page 70). Leave in place for 2 to 3 weeks.

For a large bird

• Fold the fractured wing into its natural position. In order to keep the damaged wing firmly against the body, wrap a figure-of-eight bandage around the wing, then apply another bandage over the damaged wing to pass under the sound wing and around the body several times (see diagram page 71).

Right: One method of immobilising the fractured wing of a small bird is to wrap a bandage firmly over the damaged wing and around the body.

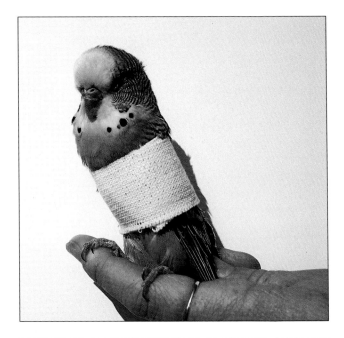

Right: Both the damaged and undamaged wings are bandaged in this alternative method of immobilising a wing fracture.

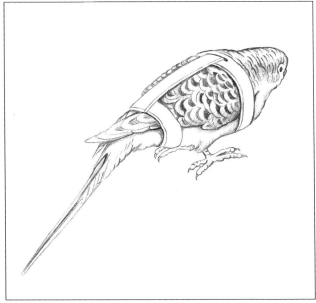

Left: A figure-of-eight bandage holds a fractured wing in place for a large bird then another bandage is wrapped over the damaged wing, around the body and under the sound wing.

Below: A drooping wing can indicate a possible fracture.

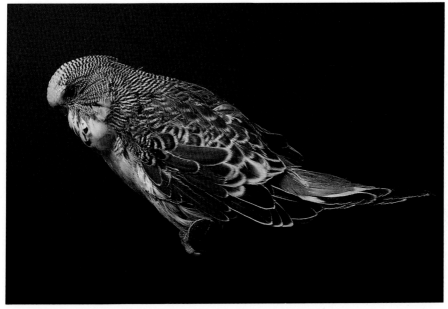

BEAK
FRACTURE
Signs

• Tip of beak broken off.
• Beak split or cracked.
• Degree of difficulty in eating, which may eventually lead to starvation.
• Fractures of the upper beak usually involve the end of the beak being broken. Fractures of the lower beak are usually down the midline.

Action

• Take the bird to the veterinarian, who may anaesthetise the bird, drill a hole in each fractured section and compress them together using nylon or wire threaded through the holes.
• If confident and dextrous, you can use superglue if the fractured ends of the beak can be very closely opposed. The difficulty of using this method is in holding the fractured ends together while the glue dries. Ensure the bird does not inhale glue fumes as they are toxic and, if excessive, may prove fatal. To avoid toxic inhalations, do not use excess glue and do not hold the glue near the bird's nostrils or beak.

FOLLOW-UP
FOR ALL
FRACTURES

• Once the fracture is immobilised, take the bird to the veterinarian to confirm:
- The fracture is correctly immobilised.
- There is no impairment to circulation.
- The skin is not broken at the fracture site. If the skin is broken, your veterinarian will prescribe a course of antibiotics.

Heatstroke

Prolonged heatstroke can lead to coma, brain damage or death.

Signs

• Bird panting, beak open, gasping for air, initially the wings held away from the body.
• Distressed, uncontrolled and agitated movement.
• Often unable to perch or stand.

Action

• Cool the bird immediately by:
- Dabbing or spraying with cool water.
- Placing the bird in front of a fan.
- Administering cool water by eye dropper or syringe.
- Administering cool water by crop tube if you are an experienced handler.

Caution

• Handle the bird as little as possible as further stress could precipitate death.
• Be careful not to chill the bird when cooling. Stop the cooling process when the bird no longer displays any signs of heatstroke (see above), or when the bird's temperature reaches 40°C (104°F) (see page 44).

Prevention

• Do not leave the bird confined in a poorly ventilated area in hot weather, for example, exposed directly to the sun behind closed glass windows.
• Provide a cool, shady area with access to cool water in very hot weather.
• Take care if transporting birds by car in hot weather. Try to travel at night or in the early morning. Open the windows of the car a little way for ventilation and use the air-conditioner if the vehicle is equipped with one.

Hypothermia
(Low Body Temperature)

• A bird's normal body temperature is between 40°C (104°F) and 42°C (108°F).
• Many species of birds are born featherless, such as members of the parrot family. Featherless nestlings are more susceptible to hypothermia, especially if they are orphaned.
• Debilitated birds are susceptible to hypothermia.

Signs

• An adult bird fluffs up the feathers.
• Often the bird is on the bottom of the cage.
• Weakness.
• Body (cloacal) temperature of 38°C (100°F) or less.

Action

• Slow, gentle warming. Take care not to warm the bird too rapidly as this can lead to shock and death.
• Place the bird on a hot water bottle adequately covered to prevent burning. Alternatively, place the bird near an electric heater, a 60 watt incandescent light bulb or on an electric heating pad (see page 45).

Caution

• Dry heat can cause dehydration. Increase the humidity by placing a shallow bowl of water in the cage or between the heat source and the bird.
• Always check the intensity of the heat and the period of time the bird should be exposed to it, knowing that you only want to warm the bird.
• When a bird is sufficiently warm, the feathers will be smooth and unruffled and the bird will be alert and active. If necessary, the body (cloacal) temperature can be checked (see page 44).

Laboured Breathing

• Unlike humans, birds have a system of air sacs in their chest and abdomen linked to the lungs and skeletal system. These air sacs assist birds in flight.
• Any infection of the respiratory system is very dangerous because it can spread throughout the body via the air sacs.
• It is difficult to detect the chest movement of healthy birds as they breathe.
• Healthy birds may pant with their beak open in very hot weather.

Causes

Laboured breathing may be caused by:
• Hot weather.
• Infection.
• Parasites.
• Shock.

Signs

• Breathing rapid and shallow or slow and deep.
• The bird's beak may be open.
• Poor exercise tolerance and reluctance to move.
• Noisy breathing, such as wheezing and clicking.
• Fluffed up.
• Coughing.
• Poor appetite.

Action

• Handle the bird as little as possible.
• Place the bird in a quiet, warm (30°–32°C (86°–90°F)) environment with subdued lighting.
• Make sure water is available.
• Clean the bird's nostrils of any nasal discharge:
- If the discharge is dry and adhering to the nostrils, remove using tweezers (forceps).
- If the discharge is watery, wipe away with a moist cotton bud (swab).

• Isolate the bird. Many respiratory diseases are highly contagious to other birds, and a few, such as psittacosis, are contagious to humans.
• Contact your veterinarian.

Caution

• Laboured breathing may be the sign of a life-threatening problem.

Orphan Bird

Young birds are broadly classified into nestlings and fledglings.
• **Nestlings.** Stay in the nest, are unable to fly and cannot procure food. They are fed by the parent(s).
• **Fledglings.** Can leave and return to the nest. At first their flight may be for a short distance and is not well coordinated. Their food may be supplemented by the parent(s).

Young birds may also be classified according to certain characteristics at birth, namely:
• **Precocial.** They are born covered in down, are able to walk and self-feed and leave the nest following the parent(s). They only need the parent(s) for warmth and security — for example, ducklings and chickens.
• **Altricial.** They are born featherless, cannot walk and the eyes are closed. They are fed by the parent(s) — for example, budgerigars.

CARE OF PRECOCIAL ORPHANS

• **Temperature.** House the young orphan in a cardboard box lined with shredded newspaper. Place a 40 watt light bulb above the box, sufficiently high to maintain the floor temperature within the box at 30°–32°C (86°–90°F). Check the temperature by placing a thermometer on the floor of the box, directly under the heat source. Provide space for the chick to move away from the heat

76

source to prevent overheating. Gradually reduce the temperature to 20°C (68°F) by moving the light bulb further away as the chick becomes feathered.

• **Feeding.** Sprinkle crumbled chick-starter pellets throughout the bedding and provide whole pellets for consumption from a suitable dispenser. A special water dispenser should also be provided so that fresh water is freely available while there is no danger of the young bird falling in the water.

CARE OF ALTRICIAL ORPHANS

• **Temperature.** House the young orphan in a cardboard box lined with shredded newspaper. Place a 40 watt light bulb above the box, sufficiently high to maintain the floor temperature within the box at 30°–32°C (86°–90°F). Check the temperature by placing a thermometer on the floor of the box directly under the heat source. Provide space for the chick to move away from the heat source to prevent overheating. Gradually reduce the temperature to 20°C (68°F) by moving the light bulb further away as the chick becomes feathered.

• **Feeding.** Feed the chick hourly. Orphan birds can eat the same food as adults except it must be of an appropriate consistency. A slurry is a thin paste made by adding water to solid food to create a fluid consistency. Feed small amounts frequently, allowing the crop to empty between feeds. When the crop is full, there is a swelling on the side of the neck. Most altricial breeds gape for food, an instinctive response that can be stimulated by touching the orphan's beak or top of the head. Blunt tweezers, syringe, eye dropper or spoon can be used to place food in the orphan's mouth. At this stage, sufficient water is obtained through the food.

SUGGESTED DIETS

Grain eaters such as cockatoos, canaries and budgerigars

• Add 3 teaspoons of water to 3 teaspoons of rearing mix and feed as a slurry (thin paste).

• If feeding by syringe, add sufficient water so that the slurry (thin paste) can be sucked up into the syringe.

Carnivores such as birds of prey
• Add water to tinned cat or dog food to make a paste.
• Add water to dry cat or dog food and feed as a slurry (thin paste).
• Chicken or rabbit flesh broken up into small pieces provides a more solid type of diet.

Nectivores such as lorikeets
• Mix crushed plain biscuits and rolled oats with honey, then add water to form a slurry (thin paste).

Omnivores such as crows and magpies
• Blend together chicken, hard-boiled (hard-cooked) egg, wholegrain (whole wheat) bread and tinned cat or dog food to a porridge-like consistency.

Insectivores such as wrens and wagtails
• Mix together crumbled hard-boiled (hard-cooked) egg, cheese, tinned cat or dog food, wholegrain (whole wheat) bread and water and feed as a slurry (thin paste).

Unidentified orphan
• A suitable diet is 2 parts tinned cat or dog food, 1 part mashed hard-boiled (hard-cooked) egg, 1 part cooked spinach (silverbeet) and 1 to 2 drops of a multivitamin supplement. Add water and feed as a slurry (thin paste).

Opposite (top):
Precocial birds are born covered in down, are able to walk and self-feed.

Opposite (bottom):
Altricial birds are born featherless, cannot walk and their eyes are closed.

Do you know?

There are no nectivores in the U.K.

Poisoning

• Birds are poisoned by inhalation, ingestion or absorption of toxic substances.
• Caged birds in the home are often poisoned by inhalation of contaminated air, such as fumes from cooking oil and burning fat in the kitchen, carbon monoxide emission from the family car, fresh house

Causes

paint and insecticidal and herbicidal sprays used in the home and garden.
• Carnivorous birds may be poisoned by eating animals that have been poisoned in an eradication program.
• Insectivorous birds may be poisoned by eating insects that have been poisoned with an insecticidal agent.
• Grain-eating birds may be poisoned by eating grain contaminated deliberately or accidentally with a poisonous substance.

Signs

• The common signs are:
- Vomiting.
- Diarrhea.
- Lethargy.
- Depression.
- Convulsions.
- Twitching.
- Staggering.
- Coma.
• Only one or a few of these signs may be evident because they vary according to the type of poison, the quantity ingested and the length of time the bird has been poisoned.

Action

Caution

• Contact your veterinarian and describe the signs if you are not sure what has poisoned your bird. In some cases the veterinarian can give the bird a specific antidote.
• Some countries have poison information centres which can provide assistance.
• Initiate treatment *if you are sure* that the bird has been poisoned and you have identified the poison involved.

If the bird's feathers and skin are contaminated with a poisonous substance

• Wash the bird with warm water and soap, then rinse with plain warm water several times. Keep the bird warm (see page 45).

If the bird has ingested an unknown poison

• The general treatment is to give water using an eye dropper or syringe.

If the bird has ingested acid

• Give sodium bicarbonate (baking soda) solution. Mix up ½ teaspoon of sodium bicarbonate (baking soda) in a cup of water. Using an eye dropper or syringe, administer 6 to 20 drops depending on the size of the bird.

If the bird has ingested kerosene or phenol

• Give a few drops of olive oil by mouth.

If the bird is convulsing intermittently

• Wait until the convulsions stop then take the bird to your veterinarian.
• To prevent injury to itself, wrap the bird in a towel and place in a container for transport to your veterinarian (see page 21).

If the bird is convulsing continuously

• Try to stop the bird injuring itself by wrapping in a towel.
• Contact your veterinarian and take the bird to the surgery as quickly as possible (see page 21), together with a sample of the suspected poison if available.

Using the poisons table

To use the following table, you must be sure that the bird has been poisoned and know what poison is involved before giving treatment. If uncertain, contact a veterinarian or poison information centre immediately.

SPECIFIC TREATMENT FOR POISONS FOUND IN THE HOME AND GARDEN

Poison	Sources
Alcohol/Methylated spirits	Bird may be offered alcohol by an irresponsible person.
Arsenic (vermin, poisons, insecticides, herbicides)	Ingestion of grass sprayed or rodents poisoned wi arsenical preparations; preening feathers covered with insecticidal or herbicidal spray.
Benzine hexachloride (Lindane, Dieldrin, Aldrin, Chlordane, Gammexane)	Insecticidal rinse absorbed through skin.
Carbon monoxide	Car exhaust fumes; exposed to fumes.
Chlorine	Concentrated powder or tablet used in swimming pools; chlorinated swimming pool water is not poisonous.
Kerosene	Heating fuel and cleaning fluid which has a burnin effect on bird's skin; preens affected area thereby ingesting kerosene orally.
Lead	Bird poisoned by preening feathers contaminated with lead.

igns *(in order of onset or severity)*	Treatment
epression; vomiting; wobbling; collapse.	Give water; keep warm (see page 45); contact your veterinarian.
ʰirsty; vomiting; fluid diarrhea with blood; ollapse; death.	Contact your veterinarian immediately.
gitated; restless; twitching; convulsions; ɔma; death.	If no sign of convulsions, wash with soap and water and rinse thoroughly; contact your veterinarian.
ɔgs wobbly; breathing difficult.	Remove from poisonous environment to fresh air; contact your veterinarian immediately who can administer oxygen directly to lungs and give a respiratory stimulant.
eeping red eye; red mouth; ulcerations mouth and tongue; vomiting; diarrhea.	Rinse eyes and mouth with water; encourage bird to drink water; contact your veterinarian.
ɔd, inflamed skin; inflamed and ɔerated tongue; vomiting; diarrhea; ɔssible convulsions.	Wash bird with soap and water; give 2–3 drops of olive oil; contact your veterinarian.
ɔor appetite; weight loss; vomiting; arrhea. Depending on degree of ɔd poisoning, bird may show signs of ʌperexcitability, convulsions, depression, ɔndness, paralysis, coma.	Lead poisoning shows up over a period of time. Consult your veterinarian who will confirm lead poisoning by a blood test.

SPECIFIC TREATMENT FOR POISONS FOUND IN THE HOME AND GARDEN

Poison	Sources
Metaldehyde	Snail and slug poison in powder or pellet form.
Oil	Oil spill.
Organo-phosphate carbomate	Snail and slug poison in pellet form.
Warfarin	The bird may eat the poison itself or eat a dead rat that has been poisoned with warfarin, a substance which stops blood from clotting.
Zinc	Zinc contained in new galvanised wire cage or aviary.

igns *(in order of onset or severity)*	Treatment
emor; diarrhea; wobbling; convulsions.	Contact your veterinarian immediately.
overed in oil; depressed.	Wash with warm water and soap; if unable to remove oil see your veterinarian.
emor; diarrhea; wobbling; convulsions.	Contact your veterinarian immediately.
ethargy; weakness; laboured breathing; ay be signs of haemorrhage; collapse; eath. Signs may be slow to develop and ary according to time and amount gested.	If recently ingested see your veterinarian who can administer an antidote; recovery rate very good.
omiting and diarrhea; may be signs blood.	See your veterinarian who can administer the antidote calcium EDTA.

Shock

- Shock usually results from some physical or emotional trauma, for example, being terrorised by a cat, and may be associated with blood loss, infection, poison (see page 79) or dehydration (see page 55).
- Shock may range from mild to severe, and can bring about total collapse, coma and death.
- Handling a bird that is in a state of shock may aggravate the shock and cause death.
- Birds are more susceptible to shock than dogs and cats.

Signs

- The bird's feathers are fluffed up and the bird is usually down on the floor of the cage or aviary.
- Rapid, shallow breathing.
- Head may be turned towards the wing with the eyes partly closed.
- The bird is weak and does not resist being caught.

Action

- Minimal handling.
- Control any bleeding.
- Place the bird in a warm (30°–32°C (86°–90°F)), quiet, secluded, humid, dimly lit environment (see page 45).
- If the bird's state of shock has not improved within approximately 3 hours, contact your veterinarian.
- When the bird's condition improves, any minor injuries can be treated. Life-threatening injuries must be treated immediately they are observed (see page 25).

Starvation

- Starvation is generally associated with wild birds. In most cases it is due to an injury, for example, a bird with a broken wing cannot fly to feeding grounds and a bird with a broken beak cannot eat.

• Feel the breast of the bird. If the breast (keel) bone is obvious and prominent to the touch and there is wastage of breast (pectoral) muscles, this indicates the bird is suffering from starvation and/or some other illness.

• Handle the bird gently and as little as possible to prevent shock.
• Allow the bird to rest in a warm, dark environment for an hour or so before attempting any feeding.
• The type of food given to the bird will vary according to the species (see page 76).
• If the bird will not eat, force-feed with fluids (water and honey or glucose mixture) from a syringe or eye dropper.
• Some birds will not feed from the ground. Use blunt-ended tweezers (forceps) to place the food in the bird's mouth.

Stress

Healthy birds are more likely to survive stressful situations whereas sick birds are more likely to succumb.

• Stress may be caused by one factor or the interaction of several factors, such as confinement in a small or poorly designed cage that does not allow the bird to fly, overcrowding, harassment by predators, exposure to climatic extremes, and excessive or rough handling.

• There are various levels of stress.
• Signs of a bird suffering acute stress, such as that caused by rough handling:
- Eyes partially closed.
- The bird goes limp in the hand.
- Collapse.
• Signs of a chronic level of stress, such as that caused by overcrowding:

- Poor appetite.
- Weight loss.
- Lethargy.
- Feather-plucking.
- Self-mutilation.

Action

• Remove the bird from the cause of stress.
• Acute stress may lead to shock (see page 86).
• Overcrowding may cause feather-plucking by other birds. Remove the affected bird and clean any blood from the feathers. Wounds should be allowed to heal completely before returning the bird to companions.
• If feather loss is the result of self-mutilation, check the bird for parasites such as lice and mites. See your veterinarian. Self-plucking can be very difficult to stop and often requires veterinary expertise and treatment.

Prevention

• Ensure the cage is of suitable size and shape for the particular bird.
• Avoid excessive or rough handling. Handling of shocked, ill or injured birds should be kept to an absolute minimum.
• Cages and aviaries should be designed and positioned to protect birds from the elements and predators.
• Avoid overcrowding.
• Boredom may lead to self-mutilation. Provide the bird with a companion and/or suitable entertainment, for example, mirrors, bells, ladders.

Vomiting

Unlike humans, vomiting can be a normal part of a bird's behaviour. For example, birds of prey vomit undigestible material such as bones. Budgerigars may vomit as part of their courtship behaviour. However, vomiting may be a sign of a problem, especially if associated with lethargy, not eating and diarrhea.

Causes

• Ingestion of foreign material.
• Mouldy food.
• Infection.
• Crop injury and/or obstruction.
• Overeating.
• Poisoning.
• Kidney failure.

Signs

• While you may not observe the bird vomiting, an obvious sign is the matting of feathers around the bird's head with what looks like a tacky mucus and partially digested food or seed. Also, the vomit may be adhering to the interior of the cage.

Action

• Keep the bird warm (see page 45), remove any food from the cage and make sure water is available.
• Take the bird to your veterinarian as the causes of vomiting are numerous and the diagnosis of some of the causes can only be made by pathology and/or X-ray.

Wounds

• The most common types of wounds are puncture and laceration.
• Wounds are commonly caused by a piece of wire jutting out in the cage, an attack by another bird or cat, a gunshot or the bird flying into objects.

PUNCTURE WOUND

A puncture wound is generally painful and may or may not be accompanied by bleeding.

Action

• Carefully pluck the feathers away from the puncture hole by holding tightly to the base of the feather with

89

your fingers or a tweezer (forceps) and pulling quickly.
• Gently and carefully check the wound to see that no foreign body is embedded.
• Clean the area with 1% hydrogen peroxide and dab the wound with tincture of iodine.
• If the wound starts to bleed, apply pressure using a clean finger, with or without a gauze pad, for approximately one minute.
• If the puncture appears to penetrate through the skin into the underlying tissue, take the bird to your veterinarian who will administer antibiotics and if necessary drain the wound.

LACERATION WOUND

The wound edges are often irregular, jagged and gaping. Sometimes whole sections of the skin and underlying tissue are torn away. A laceration is usually not painful and haemorrhage is variable.

Action

• Carefully pluck the feathers away from the wound edges (see above).
• Thoroughly clean the wound with warm water or 1% hydrogen peroxide.
• Remove any feathers, dead tissue or foreign bodies from the wound.
• Apply antibiotic powder.
• See your veterinarian as the laceration may need to be stitched.
• If unable to be stitched and thus remaining open, clean the wound only if it is discharging or contaminated.
• If the bird pecks the wound excessively, apply an Elizabethan collar (see page 40).
• Keep the bird confined in a small area to restrict movement until the wound has practically healed.

Above (left and right): Self-mutilation and feather-plucking may result from stress, triggered by boredom and overcrowding.

Left: Feathers around the head matted with tacky mucus and partially digested food indicate vomiting.

INDEX

ACKNOWLEDGMENTS

I would like to thank my wife Jan and children Melanie, Samantha, Damien and Edwina for being so patiently supportive during the time of writing.

My sincere thanks to my father Eric for his diligent assistance in planning, researching and proofreading, and also to my sister Judy Shields for undertaking the daunting task of deciphering my notes and transferring them to print.

I would also like to thank my partner Dr David Lonergan and the staff of Gordon Veterinary Hospital — Dr Andrew Morgan, Dr Sue McMillan and the nurses, Jenifer Reber, Kim Tupper and Diane Spalding — for their kindly advice and generous spirit of co-operation.

Finally, I am grateful to Joe and Val Picone for allowing me to take photographs in their Ryde Aviaries.

TIM HAWCROFT